WOMEN AND THE WORD

The Madeleva Lecture series annually commemorates the opening of the Center For Spirituality of Saint Mary's College, Notre Dame, Indiana, and honors the memory of the woman who inaugurated the college's pioneering program in theology, Sister Madeleva, C.S.C.

WOMEN AND THE WORD

*The Gender of God in the New Testament
and the Spirituality of Women*

SANDRA M. SCHNEIDERS

1986 Madeleva Lecture
in Spirituality

PAULIST PRESS
New York/Mahwah

To
my Mother
and the memory of my Father (1909–1968)
with love and gratitude

ISBN: 0–8091–2802–0

Published by Paulist Press
997 Macarthur Blvd.
Mahwah, N.J. 07430

Printed and bound in the United States of America

WOMEN AND THE WORD

The Gender of God in the New Testament and the Spirituality of Women

I. THE QUESTION ABOUT THE GENDER OF GOD

A. *The Modernity of the Question*

Sister Mary Madeleva, CSC, in whose honor this lecture is being presented, had two abiding passions which gave shape to her life and to which this College, St. Mary's, is a lasting testimony. First, she was devoted to American young women. Second, she was devoted to education in general and to theological education in particular. Observing in the 1940's that the teaching of religion from grade school through college was woefully inadequate and that there were no graduate schools of theology open to the laity, mostly women, who taught religion, Sister Madeleva inaugurated the first graduate school of theology for the laity. The Graduate Program in Sacred

Theology and Scripture, begun here at St. Mary's in 1943, was eventually approved by the Vatican and served as a model and resource for Regina Mundi, the first theological faculty for women in Rome. With a pride that would befit any feminist of today, Sister Madeleva closes her account of the beginning of theological education for women with these words, "Once St. Thomas [Aquinas] might have had to prove that women have souls. Now he can regard happily their Thomistic minds and the home in which they honor his *Summa*."[1]

If she were alive today I suspect Sister Madeleva would understand very well why many young and not so young women are exercised by the theological question of the gender of God. And I am certain that she would want the question addressed with unflinching honesty and theological rigor. This attempt to define the problem raised by the traditional ascription of masculinity to God and to suggest some ways of resolving it which are both faithful to the tradition and liberating for women is dedicated to the memory of Sister Mary Madeleva, an American woman religious who was such a gift to her own age because she was so well ahead of her time.

At the outset of this discussion it is important to be aware that the question of the gender of God is a thoroughly modern issue. No matter how entrenched in the imagination of the average Christian the image of a male God might be, theological tradition has never assigned sex to God.[2] St. Gregory of Nazianzus well represented the tradition when he affirmed that the terms "Father" and "Son" as applied to the persons of the Trinity were not names of natures or essences but of relations[3] and even in this case the terms are used metaphorically. In other words, God is neither a father nor a son but the first person of the Trinity is related to the second person as origin is related to that which is originated. Because the ancients believed that God was indeed personal, and because their defective biology ascribed all agency in procreation or personal originating activity to the male partner, their choice of "father" for the originating person of the Trinity was logical enough. And since they wished to affirm the absolute likeness and equality of the one originated to the divine principle they called the second person the "son." They were, however, quite aware of the metaphorical nature of their language and never intended to impute actual sexuality to the God whom Scripture affirms is pure Spirit (cf. Jn 4:24).

Second, theological tradition has virtually always maintained that the maleness of Jesus is theologically, christologically, soteriologically, and sacramentally irrelevant.[4] It has been suggested, not without reason, that the attempt of the Vatican's Congregation for the Doctrine of the Faith in its "Declaration on the Question of the Admission of Women to the Ministerial Priesthood" (*Inter Insignores*)[5] to assign theological significance to the sex of Jesus by maintaining that women Christians, because they are female, do not resemble Christ is not only non-traditional but also at least theologically confused if not strictly heretical.[6] As patristics scholar R.A. Norris states,

> The argument [against the ordination of women on the grounds that male sex is required for likeness to Christ] is virtually unprecedented. It does not in fact state any of the traditional grounds on which ordination to the presbyterate or episcopate has been denied to women. To accept this argument and its practical consequences, therefore, is not to maintain tradition but to alter it by altering its meaning.[7]

More important, however, than its non-traditionality is the threat it raises to a central theological affirmation about the incarnation, namely, that as Gregory of Nazianzus and numerous other Fathers of the Church have maintained, *"Tò gàr apróslēpton atherápeuton,"* i.e.,"What is not assumed is not redeemed."[8] The Vatican argument attempts to make the maleness of Jesus a necessary precondition to his being who he is, God-with-us, and doing what he does, redeeming us by his paschal mystery. To do so,

4

as Norris says, "is to qualify or deny the universality of his redemption."[9]

In short, the theological tradition of the Church never assigned sex to God and almost never (until the theologically faulty 1977 document) assigned any theological significance to the sex of Jesus. Why, then, is the gender of God such a troubling question for contemporary Christians, especially for women whose consciousness has been raised by the women's movement in our time?

B. The Dilemma for Women

[As women have become aware of their inferior status and actual oppression in family, society, and Church, they have also become aware that the gender of God, God's presumed masculinity, has functioned as the ultimate religious legitimation of the unjust social structures which victimize women.] First, the maleness of Jesus has been used in Christian cultures as a support from divine revelation for the age-old claim that maleness is normative for humanity and that men are superior to women. Most western languages themselves, in which the generic human is always masculine, testify incessantly to the misconception that humanity is originally and normatively male and that women are a derivative and subordinate, if not actually misbegotten, version of the essentially male species. Male privilege, based on this erroneous assumption of male superiority, is firmly entrenched in virtually every sector of human life.

Second, the "fatherhood" of God has been used to justify patriarchy or father-rule, the social system which sacralizes male domination and legitimates virtually all forms of oppression of the weak by the strong. We will return to the topic of patriarchy shortly.

Third, the masculinity of God and of Jesus has been used, in the practical sphere, to deny the likeness of women to God and to Christ and to exclude them from full participation in the life of the Church. Whether this spiritual degradation takes the relatively mild form of excluding little girls from serving at the altar or the more serious forms of exclusion of women from decision-making positions in the Church and enforcement of their sacramental dependence on men, it has a destructive effect on women's spiritual self-image and perverts their relationships with male Christians and with God.

The masculinity of God, in other words, is not primarily an issue in speculative theology. It can easily be established that the God of Judaeo-Christian revelation and Christian theological tradition is not male and that Jesus' maleness is theologically irrelevant. This helps very little, however, because the real problem is not in the area of systematic theology but in the area of religious experience or spirituality.[10] How women experience themselves in relation to God, Christ, and Church is profoundly affected by the imputed masculinity of God which is operative in the imaginations of both male and female believers.

Once their consciousness is raised, women Christians can find themselves impaled on the horns of a dilemma. Either they can continue as Christians, accepting the spiritual consequences of their lack of resemblance to God and Christ and their consequent inferiority to and spiritual dependence on men in the Church (the position advocated by the Vatican Declaration despite its protestations to the contrary), or they can abandon Christianity as a hopelessly patriarchal religion and seek their spiritual home in a religious tradition in which women and women's experience are central and valued.[11] Unless educated and aware women can find a creative and liberating understanding of God and of Jesus, one which does not glorify masculinity at the expense of femininity and does not justify the oppression of women by men, they have no future in institutional Christianity.

II. Preliminary Clarifications

Before undertaking an exploration of the problem of God's "masculinity" and women's spirituality two clarifications are necessary. First, we must distinguish clearly between sex and gender because, as we will see, it is the *gender* of God and the *sex* of Jesus which are the real problems. Second, we have to distinguish between patriarchy (and paternalism) on the one hand and paternity or fatherhood on the other because it is only the former which is problematic. Fatherhood as such, provided that it is not used exclusively, is one appropriate metaphor for God.

A. Sex and Gender

Sex refers to biological identity, the possession of male or female sexual organs and the proportionate activity of male or female hormones which grounds the distinctive roles of men and women in the reproductive process. Gender, however, refers to the experience of self and others in terms of sexual identity. Although sex and gender normally coincide in humans, i.e., females experience themselves and are experienced by others as feminine and males as masculine, this is not always the case, nor is the experience always totally dichotomous. Thus, someone who is biologically a male might experience himself as feminine and might be experienced that way by others. And persons are sometimes experienced as both feminine and masculine, or androgynous. The point is that while sex is biologically determined by observation of empirically available data, gender refers to the way one experiences oneself or others.[12]

God, as we have said, is neither male nor female, i.e., God does not have a body and therefore does not have sex. But because all human persons have gender and we experience God as personal we tend to experience God anthropomorphically as either masculine or feminine or both, i.e., as male and female successively, or as androgynous. Our God-image, as we will explain below, is a function of the imagination, and the Christian religious imagination is deeply influenced by the belief in the personal nature of God, by the overwhelmingly male God-language in the Bible, and by the incarnation of God in the concrete humanity of a male human being, Jesus. Until very recently many if not most Christians, including those who were theologically convinced that God is Spirit, experienced God as almost exclusively masculine. Theologically well-informed people of both sexes have insisted vehemently on the maintenance of exclusively male language for God in public prayer.[13] To a large extent this insistence has more to do with maintaining male dominant power arrangements in family, society, and Church than with theological issues. But for many people the problem is genuinely religious. Their problem is a paralysis of the religious imagination. To imagine God or speak to God as feminine does not simply change the God image for these people; it destroys it.

If God is pure Spirit, the same cannot be said about Jesus who was actually a male. However, although biologically male and masculine in gender, Jesus has also been experienced as distinctly feminine in many ways. Sentimental art provides a perverted testimony to this fact, but the motherhood of Jesus and of Christ is a consistent theme in medieval mystical literature. Bernard of Clairvaux, Julian of Norwich, Anselm of Canterbury, Gertrude of Helfta, Mechtild of Hackeborn, and Mechtild of Magdeburg are among the spiritual writers whose works are explored by medieval scholar Caroline Walker Bynum in her 1982 volume, *Jesus as Mother*.[14] The Gospel portrays Jesus as non-aggressive, non-competitive, meek and humble of heart, a nurturer of the weak, and a friend of the outcast. He manifested and preached a spirituality that was characterized by stereotypically feminine rather than masculine virtues. This femininity of Jesus has often enough proven difficult for men to assimilate, but it has always supported the spirituality of women. For women, the problem is not the gender of Jesus, his masculinity which is so inclusively feminine, but his sex. It is the biological fact that Jesus, by being a man rather than a woman, is irreducibly and irrevocably different from women that seems to exclude women from the fullness of identity with him. Furthermore, the maleness of Jesus cannot help but intensify the experience of God as masculine and of maleness as normative, i.e., as the best and fullest way to be human.

B. Patriarchy and Paternity

A second distinction important for our purposes is that between paternity on the one hand and patriarchy/paternalism on the other. Patriarchy is a social system based on the *patria potestas,* i.e., the absolute and unaccountable power over wives and concubines, children, servants, slaves, animals and real property enjoyed by the *paterfamilius,* i.e., the father who is head of the family, tribe, or clan. To the father of the family belonged, as property, all members of the extended household and all goods. In classical Greek and Roman societies this authority of ownership extended even to the power of life and death. Children, especially girls, were often deemed valueless to the father and left to die. Insubordinate wives or slaves could be sold or killed.[15] While sons, when they became adults, were emancipated and became patriarchs in their own right, daughters were passed, with or without their consent, from the control of the father to that of a husband,[16] i.e., from one patriarch to another.

In the patriarchal system authority and power were strictly coterminous and belonged totally and exclusively to the head of the household unless he delegated it to another. The authority and power of the *paterfamilias* were considered as divinely established, and thus the patriarchal system was unalterable and rebellion against the father was rebellion against God. Furthermore, even though in the absence of a man patriarchal power might sometimes be exercised by a woman, e.g., by a mother or a queen, and unemancipated males, e.g., minor sons and slaves, were as subject to the father's dominion as were females in the family, there is a vital connection in the patriarchal system among power, authority, property, and maleness. Conversely, powerlessness, exclusion from authority, dependence, and femaleness are closely linked. And the entire system is understood as the product and expression of the will of God.

For two reasons patriarchy is not just one social system among others. First, patriarchy is the basic principle of all major relational systems in the western world. As the former president of the World Council of Churches, Dr. W.A. Visser't Hooft, expressed it:

> ... the patriarchal spirit and the doctrine upon which it is based have had an astonishingly wide influence, penetrating into many different spheres of life. Indeed, it has not been merely one of the many facets of society, but has rather formed its general pattern. ... [Thus] emancipation [from patriarchy] concerns not only developments in family life, but also those in the state, the church and even in international relations.[17]

Visser't Hooft, like Rosemary Ruether, has pointed out that patriarchy is the basic principle underlying not only the subordination of women to men, but of one race to another, of colonies to master nations, of children to adults, of nations to divine right monarchs, of believers to clergy. In other words, patriarchy is the nerve of racism, ageism, classism, colonialism, and clericalism as well as of sexism.[18] Patriarchy is fundamentally a masculine power structure in which all relationships are understood in terms of superiority and inferiority and social cohesion is assured by the exercise of dominative power.

The second reason why patriarchy is not just one system among others is that patriarchy is essentially hierarchy, i.e., the power and authority exercised over subordinates is believed to derive from the will of God and is exercised in the name of God. The patriarchal structure of the family was understood as divinely established for the good of all. When this structure was extended to other situations they were seen as quasi-families in which there is one adult and all others are minors. The feudal lord, the abbot in his monastery, the divine right monarch, the priest in his parish, the white European in the colonies, the husband in relation to his wife, the slave-holder with his "darkies," the Pope, were all father-figures caring for the "children" over which God had placed them. The difference, of course, between these extensions of patriarchy and its original locus, the family, is that these "children" are adults and, unlike real children, they are expected never to grow up. Thus, in a patriarchal system most people will remain subordinates all their lives and they cannot protest against this arrangement without challenging God "himself" who is the first patriarch and the legitimator of all others.

While not all men are patriarchs, women never are. Where patriarchy reigns women are subject to men. The man may be father, husband, slaveholder, priest, or Pope but the woman is always a minor. It is not surprising, then, that women, once they have analyzed the situation, repudiate patriarchy as the universal social structure and especially its claims to divine legitimacy. A patriarchal God, to feminist women, is at least a legitimator of women's victimization by men if not "himself" the very personification of the oppression of women.

However, it is important to distinguish sharply between patriarchy (including its more benign expression as paternalism) on the one hand, and paternity or fatherhood on the other. The association of fatherhood with patriarchy is so long-standing and widespread that the equation of the two is quite understandable and very often perfectly accurate. However, it is possible for a man to be a father to his minor children without assuming absolute power over them and to remain a father in relation to adult children whose autonomy and equality with himself he fully accepts. Likewise, it is possible for God to be experienced as paternal without being experienced as a patriarch. And a father-God who is not experienced as a patriarch can equally well be experienced as a mother-God without loss of status.

III. IMAGINATION AND SPIRITUALITY

In what has been said so far I have attempted to locate with some accuracy the problem of the gender of God. The problem is not the sex of God (which does not exist) but our experience of God as masculine; and it is not the masculinity of Jesus (who is anything but a glorification of machismo) but his male sex. However, the reason Jesus' male sex is a problem is because it is seen as a revelatory confirmation of the masculinity of

God and therefore of the divinity of maleness. Jesus, the man, is the incarnation of the Son of the Father. Consequently, our primary concern must be with the experienced masculinity of God.

God is not male; but we experience God as masculine. In other words, we imagine God anthropomorphically as male. There is a tendency, especially among those with a traditional Catholic education, to regard the imagination as a frivolous, if not dangerous, capacity for nonsense in human beings who were intended to function rationally. In recent years the work of scholars in theology,[19] liturgy,[20] and Scripture[21] has made us aware that the imagination is not primarily a reproductive or combinatory faculty but is our constructive capacity to integrate our experience into dynamic and effective wholes which then function as the interpretive grids of further experience.

Perhaps our most accessible example of the functioning and the effect of the imagination is the formation of our own self-image. The self, like God and world, is not a finite and circumscribed entity of which we can take a mental photograph. To "get the picture" of ourselves is a never-ending process of integrating our experience into our sense of subjectivity in such a way that we can experience ourselves as other than and in some relationship to everything else.

The image of the self, like the image of God

and of world, is not wholly the product of rational or deliberate processes but is a complex and dynamic reality which is formed by the interaction of conscious and unconscious factors in relation to actual experience. Once formed, the image organizes and interprets our experience so that what we actually experience as well as its meaning and significance is largely the function of our imagination. Thus, the person with a distorted self-image may be incapable of experiencing much to which she or he is actually exposed, may misinterpret what is experienced, and may draw all the wrong conclusions from it. The images of self, God, and world, furthermore, are incapable of total objectification and they are never static. We may know that our self-image is inflated, negative, or realistic but we can never say exactly what our self-image is. Furthermore, our self-image undergoes constant modification as it interacts with our experience. In other words, the work of the imagination is ongoing. We are not the passive victims of our imaginations but can affect the vital images of self, God, and world.

It is important to recognize that the three basic life-structuring images: God, self, and world, are interrelated. If world is imagined as a finite globe floating in space God may well be imagined as a finite but very powerful being living someplace in space and acting upon the world. The self, in such an imagination, is a very small creature whose basic relationship with God is one of subjection to an all-powerful world-controller. In a world which is imagined as patriarchal in fact and by divine institution, God is necessarily imagined as the supreme patriarch. A woman with such an imagination must see herself as an inferior version of humanity subject first to human men and ultimately to the infinite divine male who established the patriarchal world order. This is, in fact, the imagination which the Church has gone to great lengths to encourage in both women and men. God is presented as a great patriarch whose enormous household is this world. This patriarchal father-God enjoys absolute and unaccountable power over nature and persons. This God recognizes in his male children a certain likeness to himself and places them in charge of his female children. However, in relationship to the divine patriarch himself all his children are feminine because, in relation to him, they are powerless and dependent.

The imagination is not entirely subject to rational control. Our God, self, and world images begin to form very early and they are reinforced by our experiences at home, in school, in church, and in the broader society. These images carry such a numinous sense of reality that to interfere with them seems not only impossible but dangerous. To tamper with our images of self, God, and world threatens to destroy the very coordinates of reality. However, as we know, these images can be changed. World-images have been modified by science, by philosophy, by travel, by the arms race. And one of psychotherapy's major tasks is to heal the unhealthy self-image which paralyzes a person's capacity for life and growth. ✗

The tenacity of the patriarchal God-image is such that many feminists have decided that the only course open to women whose self-image has been healed of gender inferiority and whose world-image has been healed of hierarchy in general and patriarchy in particular is to abandon the Christian God altogether. I would like to suggest that just as the self and world images can be healed, so can the God-image. It cannot be healed, however, by rational intervention alone. Repeating the theological truth that God is Spirit may correct our ideas but a healthy spirituality requires a healing of the imagination which will allow us not only to think differently about God but to experience God differently. The imagination is accessible not primarily to abstract ideas but to language, images, interpersonal experience, symbolism, art—all the integrated approaches which appeal simultaneously to intellect, will, and feeling. What must be undertaken is a therapy of the religious imagination, first in regard to God and then in regard to our relationship with Jesus Christ.

19

IV. The "Maleness" of God In the Old Testament

The primary concern of this paper is the gender of God in the New Testament. However, in order to understand Jesus' use of God language in the New Testament it is necessary to investigate the religious tradition which shaped Jesus' own image of God, namely, that of the Hebrew Scriptures or the Old Testament.

A. *Types of Language about God in the Old Testament*

There are at least four different types of language about God in the Old Testament: literal designations, names for God, personifications of God, and metaphors for God, among which are the two with which we will be particularly concerned, namely, God as father and God as spouse.

First, there is literal language about God. It is difficult to define the term "literal." G.B. Caird, in *The Language and Imagery of the Bible*, says " . . . words are used literally when they are meant to be understood in their primary, matter-of-fact sense."[22] Literalness has little to do with whether a statement is true or whether its referent exists.[23] If I say that I saw a UFO last night I am making a literal statement. I may be lying or I may be mistaken in believing that there is such a thing as a UFO, but since I intend my statement to be taken at face value it is a literal statement.

The Old Testament contains literal claims about God. God was the liberator who brought the Hebrews out of Egypt, the covenant-maker who bound Israel and its God together at Sinai, and the restorer who brought the chastened people back from exile. These designations, which described in the most fundamental fashion who God was to and for the people of Israel and which contrasted Israel's God with all the deities of surrounding peoples, are both literal and non-sexed. Although the writers of the Bible probably had a male warrior image in their minds when they spoke of God rescuing Israel with outstretched arm and the image of a male sovereign in their minds when they spoke of the covenanting on Mount Sinai, there is nothing in these divine activities which is necessarily masculine.

Second, the Old Testament supplies names for God. I am not speaking here of role-titles such as king, shepherd, warrior, lord, and master but of personal names for God. The fundamental and most mysterious name is actually a non-name. When Moses asked God for the divine name God replied from the burning bush, "I am who I am" or "I am who I shall be" (Ex 3:14) depending on whether one translates the verb as present or future. A verb as such has no gender and the first person form of the verb has only the gender of the speaker. God's self-appellation gives no clue to the gender of the deity, but only to God's mysterious and transcendent selfhood. The further self-designation by God, "Yahweh, the God of your ancestors, the God of Abraham, the God of Isaac, and the God of Jacob" (Ex 3:15), tells us nothing about the gender of God but only about Israel's patriarchal self-understanding in terms of male rather than female ancestors. More exactly, God's self-presentation to Moses is non-metaphorical and therefore appropriately non-sexed. The tetragrammaton (yhwh), the sacred four-character name which we read as "Yahweh," is a non-pronounceable substantive probably reflecting the verb "to be."[24] Jews, to this day, out of respect for the divine name, read the tetragrammaton as *Adonai* or "Lord," thus contributing to the imagination of God as male, but there is nothing in the divine name to necessitate this masculine reading.

Third, there are two personifications of God which had special power for Old Testament and later Jews. One, Wisdom, is biblical; the other, Shekinah, is a rabbinic word derived from the Hebrew root (shākan), meaning "to dwell." Shekinah was the term used by the rabbis to speak of a recurring experience described in the Bible itself, namely, the mysterious and perceptible presence of God among the people as pillar of cloud by day and column of fire by night (Ex 13:21), as the thick cloud which enshrouded the holy mountain when God descended to speak to Moses (cf. Ex 24:15–18), as the cloud of glory which overshadowed the meeting tent (Ex 33:9–11) and filled the tabernacle (Ex 40:34–38), and finally took up its abode in the temple in Jerusalem (2 Chr 7:1–3).[25] Interestingly enough, both Wisdom and the Divine Presence are always presented as feminine both grammatically and rhetorically. We will return to the biblical figure of Wisdom in talking about the incarnation.

The personifications of God as the feminine figures of Presence and Wisdom were late developments in Israel's history. The most ancient description of Wisdom is found in the Book of Proverbs in material dating probably from the late fifth century B.C.E.[26] Other texts dealing with Wisdom are found in Sirach (Ecclesiasticus) which dates from the second century B.C.E.[27] and the Wisdom of Solomon, a first century B.C.E. work.[28] The Shekinah theology is a later rabbinic development. Both personifications, in other words, belong to the Hellenistic period and both are kept strictly identified with God or subordinate to God lest they raise any challenge to Jewish monotheism which, by this time, had been sharply differentiated from neighboring religions that involved the worship of feminine nature deities. Thus, despite the rich potential for the development of a feminine God-image which these personifications offered to the Jewish imagination, the divine feminine was severely repressed in the interests of safeguarding the oneness and transcendence of God. As psychologists from Freud to Jung have explained in sobering detail this repression has had devastating effects on the religious psychology of individual believers and in the Church as a whole.[29]

If the literal designations and the names of God are non-sexed and the personifications of God are feminine, how are we to account for the massively masculine God-image of the Old Testament? The answer is readily available for anyone who understands how language works. Theological affirmations are addressed to the intellect; they inform the mind but do little to form the imagination. The masculine God-image is due largely to the interplay between the repression of the feminine on the one hand and the use of male metaphors for God on the other. As we have tried to suggest, the repression of the feminine was due to sociological and political interests in supporting patriarchy and a theological concern to safeguard the transcendent monotheism of Israel. In the light of contemporary psychological discoveries we cannot avoid suspecting that this repression stemmed also from male fear of feminine life-power and the male need to control and dominate what men neither understood nor shared, namely, participation in the divine capacity to bring forth life.[30]

The fourth kind of God-language we find in the Old Testament is metaphor. Contrary to long-standing presentations, metaphor is not a literary decoration or straightforward and obvious comparison between two known realities. A genuine metaphor is characterized by linguistic tension between a literally absurd statement and that to which it points. The literal absurdity of the statement forces the mind to seek for meaning at a deeper level. However, the referent of religious metaphors is usually the transcendent, something of which we have no direct experience. Thus, while we recognize that the metaphorical statement is not to be taken literally, we have no access, except through the metaphor, to the real referent.[31] For example, it is literally absurd to say that God is our father. A father is a male human being who has engendered a child by sexual intercourse with a human female. Obviously, nothing in this literal definition can be applied to God who is not a human being, does not have male sexual organs, does not have intercourse with human females, and does not have children by physical generation. Since the statement "God is our father" is obviously intended to carry meaning, the mind must seek that meaning at another level. The reason we use a metaphor is that we have no other way to speak concretely of God.

The reason we use this particular metaphor is that the human experience of fatherhood (and of certain other realities) has something in common with our God-experience and we realize that by using the metaphor we can tease the mind into creative reflection on the mysterious God.

The Scriptures are filled with metaphors for God. Many are derived from inanimate nature such as sun (Ps 84:11), rock (Dt 32:15), spring (Jer 2:13), and fire (Dt 4:24). There are also animal metaphors for God such as lion (Hos 5:14), leopard, she-bear (Hos 13:7–8; Lam 3:10), and mother eagle (Dt 32:11–12). And, of course, there are numerous human metaphors for God. Some are role metaphors such as potter, builder, shepherd, hero, warrior, physician, midwife, homemaker, judge, and king. Others, such as mother, husband, and father, are relational metaphors. While the inanimate metaphors are neuter there are among the animal and human metaphors both masculine and feminine images.[32] There is no question that the male metaphors heavily outnumber the feminine ones, but the latter are sufficiently numerous and well-drawn that their consistent neglect and trivialization in the theological and homiletic tradition can only be attributed to androcentric myopia and patriarchal self-interest. Men have controlled both theology and ministry, and the story of God they have told is the one which they wanted to hear as well as the one which kept them in power.

Although metaphors give us access to God in and through our own experience and by their concreteness appeal simultaneously to mind and affections, thus shaping the imagination of God, metaphors are also dangerous. First of all, precisely because we do not have direct knowledge of God to function as a corrective, metaphors for God drawn from human experience can easily be literalized. While we are immediately aware that the personal God is not really a rock or a mother eagle, it is easy enough to imagine that God is really a king or a father.[33] A literalized metaphor paralyzes the imagination. Instead of functioning as an ever-active incentive to affective reflection on the inexhaustible mystery of the godhead, it traps the mind in a limited and therefore untrue conception of God. As theologian Sallie McFague explains, a metaphor can only function as a metaphor and thereby give us access to the mysterious if the "is," i.e., the affirmation, and the "is not," i.e., the negative qualifier, are held in tension.[34] It is equally and simultaneously true that God is, and is not, our father. If the denial is repressed the metaphor succumbs to literalism, i.e., it dies. But the literalized metaphor, like an unburied body, is not harmless to its environment, the imagination.

The second danger of religious metaphor is

that it tends to work simultaneously in two directions. We create the metaphor to say something about God; but then God seems to be saying something about the vehicle of the metaphor. Thus, if God is a king, there is a tendency to see kings as divine.[35] If God is male, then males are divine and masculinity becomes normative of humanity, the true image of God as St. Augustine maintained in an infamous passage.[36]

B. *Old Testament Metaphors for God*[37]

In the Old Testament there are numerous metaphors for God derived from human relationships. The vast majority, although not all, of the vehicles in these metaphors either are necessarily male, e.g., father or husband, or denote roles or activities which were virtually exclusively exercised by males in Israelite society. In the New Testament Jesus frequently used one of these metaphors, namely, father, at least in speaking to God and probably also in speaking about God. Fairly early in Christian history the father metaphor was literalized in religious imagination. The literalized metaphor, it must be remembered, no longer carries its "is not" but simply transfers to the referent all the characteristics of the vehicle. Thus, God the "father" came to be imagined as literally male. All the male metaphors for God in the Old Testament then tended to be drawn into this one metaphor. Since many of the Old Testament God-metaphors such as warlord and king were patriarchal the metaphorical fatherhood of God was not only literalized but patriarchalized. As both theologian Sallie McFague and biblical scholar Johanna Bos have pointed out, the literalized father metaphor for God has not only died but, in its ascription of maleness to God, it has become actually idolatrous.[38] We have created a false god and substituted "him" for the true God of Judaeo-Christian revelation.

It is highly enlightening, then, to examine the father metaphor as it actually occurs in the Old Testament. The most striking characteristic of this metaphor is how seldom it occurs. God is actually referred to as father only twelve times in the Hebrew Scriptures and never in direct address. Father is not a name for God but "a pointer to the free presence of God, which cannot be encapsulated in or manipulated by names."[39] Five of the references to God as father concern the special relation of God to the king (2 Sam 7:14; 1 Chr 17:13; Ps 89:26; 1 Chr 22:10; 28:6) and thus do not apply to the ordinary person. The other seven references (Ps 103:13; Dt 32:6, 18; Jer 3:4–5; 31:9; Is 63:16; Mal 1:6) all refer to God in the context of Israel's sin, repentance, and restoration and God's endless forgiveness.[40] The father metaphor in the Old Testament is nowhere used to present God as a patriarch dominating the people or exercising coercive power over them. On the contrary, the father metaphor is evoked precisely to describe the compassionate love of God who is like a parent spurned by ungrateful children but who is endless in patience and loving-kindness toward a rebellious people. The God who is presented as father in the Old Testament is the like the father in the New Testament parable of the prodigal son, a paternal rather than patriarchal figure who is in no way a model for or a legitimation of patriarchy.

A second important point about the parental metaphor in the Old Testament is that it is not exclusively masculine. When Israel is referred to as a child the implied parent is sometimes masculine as in Deuteronomy 1:31 where Israel is reminded that "God bore you as a man bears his son." But at other times it is feminine as in Numbers 11:12 where the exasperated Moses demands of God, "Did I conceive all this people? Did I bring them forth, that thou should say to me, 'Carry them in thy bosom . . . ?" clearly implying that God is the true mother of this people. At other times the metaphor is both masculine and feminine as in Hosea 11:1–4:

> When Israel was a child, I loved him, and
> out of Egypt I called my son. The more I
> called them the more they went from me;
> they kept sacrificing to Baals, and burning

incense to idols. Yet it was I who taught
Ephraim to walk, I took them up in my
arms; but they did not know that I healed
them. I led them with cords of compassion,
with the bands of love, and I became to them
as one who eases the yoke on their jaws, and
I bent down to them and fed them.

Thus, it is to be noted that, while they are not as
frequent as even the infrequent paternal metaphors, there are clear maternal metaphors for
God in the Old Testament as well as a pervasive
maternal climate evoked by imagery based on the
womb. In Deuteronomy 32:18 God clearly refers
to herself, in feminine language, as "the God who
gave you birth." In Isaiah 49:15 Israel is assured
that God cherishes her people with a mother's
love. In Isaiah 66:13 God says to Israel, "As one
whom his mother comforts so will I comfort you."
In Psalm 131:2 the psalmist says of reliance on
God, "I have calmed and quieted my soul, like a
child quieted at its mother's breast." As Phyllis
Trible has pointed out[41] the typical Old Testament word for the compassion of God seems to
be drawn from *rehem* the Hebrew word for
womb, suggesting that God's tenderness is that of
a mother for the child to whom she has given
birth (cf. Is 63:15; Ex 34:6).[42] In Isaiah 42:14
God compares the divine anguish to that of a
woman in the pangs of childbirth.[43]

In sum, an examination of the Old Testament father metaphor reveals that it was by no means a common, much less the preferred or only, metaphor for God, that it was never used to portray God as a patriarch in relation to the people, and that it is complemented by maternal imagery and metaphors which assure us that in no sense was the father metaphor meant to suggest that God is male[44] or that the divine parenthood is exclusively paternal.

Besides the father metaphor which, because of Jesus' use of it, exerted a powerful influence on the Christian imagination, there is one other Old Testament male metaphor for God which has had a major impact on the Christian God-image, namely, the spousal metaphor. Like the paternal metaphor which has been distorted into an exclusive and literalized support for male supremacy and patriarchy, the spousal metaphor has also exercised a perverse influence on the Christian imagination as a degradation of feminine sexuality and a justification of patriarchal marriage.

In some of the prophets, especially Jeremiah and Hosea, the relationship between God and Israel is depicted as marital union. God is the husband and Israel the wife in a marriage founded on love rather than on patriarchal authority and power. The extended metaphor is used, however, to describe the unfaithfulness of Israel to its faithful God. Israel, the wife, is a harlot. As feminist scholars have rightly pointed out, in this metaphor female sexuality is objectified and demonized. The male is assimilated to God and the female to sinful humanity.[45]

However, it must be realized that in the patriarchal culture of ancient Israel a husband could not really sin against his wife since he could do to her with impunity what he willed.[46] Marital fidelity was never absolutely required of men whereas a woman's infidelity was considered an offense against her husband's property rights. In such a culture, therefore, this metaphor could not have been structured in any other way. To make the point that God took the free initiative in choosing Israel, that God entered into a relationship of intimate love with Israel, and that Israel was unfaithful to that covenant, God had to be imaged as the husband who alone could act this way. However, in the husband role God acts not as a patriarch would have acted but as a wife would have acted. A husband who had been betrayed by his wife would at least have divorced her if he had not had her executed. A wife who had been betrayed would be expected, nevertheless, to be faithful and loving. God, in the marital metaphor, is a faithful lover who continually seeks reconciliation through the offer of forgiveness. In other words, the patriarchy of the metaphor is assumed because of the culture, but the message of the metaphor subverts patriarchy.

Furthermore, the prophetic use of the marital metaphor is not the end of the story. The metaphor of the marriage between God and Israel is only fully developed in the Canticle of Canticles. This Old Testament book was probably originally a collection of love songs celebrating the intensely erotic mutuality between a man and a woman which is fully consummated in their spiritual and physical union.[47] However, when it was admitted to the canon of the Old Testament around 90 C.E., Rabbi Aqiba declared that it was the holy of holies of the Scriptures (*Mishna Yadayim* III, 3)[48] because it described the relationship between God and Israel. Thus, the interpretation of the Song of Songs was canonized.[49] The early Church accepted this interpretation and understood the Canticle as the story of the relationship between Christ and the Church, while the mystics, beginning with Origen in the third century,[50] have consistently understood it as a description of the mystical marriage between the soul and the Word of God.

As Phyllis Trible has explained,[51] this celebration of human sexual love is completely devoid of patriarchal overtones. In fact, scholars continue to be unable to distinguish precisely between the discourse of the woman and the man.

The mutuality of their delight in one another, the totality of their self-giving, and the finality of the love itself, which seems in no way oriented toward the producing of children or the continuation of the tribe, are a celebration of equality between the man and the woman. Although the androcentric imagination of commentators has always assumed that the male lover is God and the female Israel, the Church, or the soul, there is nothing in the Canticle itself to suggest this. God might just as plausibly be represented by the woman as by the man. The prophetic metaphors of covenant relationship are concerned only with the sinfulness of Israel. But it is the Canticle of Canticles which tells the whole story.

In the 1950's a French scholar, A. Néher, wrote a remarkable theological meditation on the meaning of the marital metaphor in the Old Testament.[52] He suggested that the metaphor was so apt for the relation between God and humanity precisely because of the equality of the partners in marriage as two autonomous subjects who freely choose to relate to each other and because of the historical character of marriage which allows for mistakes and regressions, recoveries and triumphs, growth and deepening. In no other relationship do two free adults choose one another and bind themselves to one another in an eternal covenant which must take its shape from the historical experience they forge together.

There can be no doubt that the people of the Old Testament understood marriage as a patriarchal structure in which the male was dominant and the female subordinate. We have come to understand, largely because of the Gospel presentation of Jesus' relationships with women, that patriarchy is not only not essential to marriage but is a deformation of it. The Old Testament, almost in spite of itself, has given us in the Canticle of Canticles a picture of human love that is a worthy metaphor of the divine-human relationship. It is that metaphor which must be allowed to shape our imagination while we take from the prophetic literature its point, namely, that human infidelity is the only thing that can separate us from a loving God, without literalizing its presentation of sex roles.

This brief exploration of the Old Testament language about God and the way this language has been used suggests several conclusions. God is not presented in the Old Testament in exclusively male terms. Even the two necessarily male metaphors, father and husband, are balanced by maternal imagery and the presentation of marital love as a relation of mutuality between equals. It is true that male imagery for God predominates, but this should serve to draw our attention to the unexpected feminine imagery which is perhaps more revelatory precisely because it cannot be adequately explained by the culture. In any case, any literalizing of God metaphors results not only in an impoverishment and distortion of the religious imagination but in a blasphemous assimilation of God to human categories and an idolatrous divinizing of human maleness.

V. Jesus' Experience and Presentation of God

Having examined the Old Testament presentation of God and established that it does not present God in exclusively male images and does not use either the father metaphor or the spouse metaphor to sanction patriarchy, we are in a position to examine Jesus' presentation of God in the New Testament. The established fact[53] that Jesus' preferred address for God was "Abba," the caritative form of "Father," raises two questions. Did Jesus experience God and therefore present God as exclusively masculine? Did Jesus intend to present God in patriarchal terms? If the answer to either question is affirmative, the New Testament has little to offer to women.

The first question concerns Jesus' experience of and consequent presentation of God. It is clear from the New Testament that Jesus used male images and metaphors for God. He presented God as a king who gave a wedding feast for his son (Mt 22:1–14), as a shepherd seeking a lost sheep (Lk 15:3–7), as a farmer sowing seed (Mk 4:3–9), as a father giving commands to his sons (Mt 21:28–32).

But Jesus also presented God in feminine images and metaphors. He insisted that a person must be born anew in order to enter into the reign of God. Nicodemus, with whom Jesus used this metaphor, understood it to be feminine because he asked how one could enter a second time into the maternal womb. When Jesus clarified the source of the new life, water and the Holy Spirit, he did not change the metaphor but repeated that one must indeed be born again. He even amplified the feminine image by explaining that what is born of flesh is flesh, i.e., what is born of woman is human, whereas what is born of the Spirit is divine. The divine mother of whom believers are born is the one God who is Spirit (cf. Jn 3:1–7). Unfortunately, the theological tradition which has controlled the reading of Scripture has insisted on its own male understanding of God to the extent that it has virtually obliterated from the religious imagination this clearly feminine presentation of God the Spirit as mother.[54]

A second clearly feminine God-metaphor occurs in Luke's Gospel. Jesus told two parallel parables about the merciful forgiveness of God. In one he presented God in the masculine image of a shepherd who left ninety-nine sheep in the desert to go in search of one sheep which had strayed (Lk 15:3–7). In the other, Jesus presents God in the feminine image of a woman householder who put aside the nine coins she had to search diligently for the one coin she had lost (Lk 15:8–10). The parallel endings of the two parables, the great rejoicing in heaven over the lost one that has been found, makes perfectly clear the intent of Jesus that both parables be understood as presentations of God. In view of the fact that the parables are clearly parallel and that modern people can much more easily identify from their own experience with a person searching for lost money than with a shepherd searching for a sheep it seems strange that most Christians readily identify the shepherd as God but do not see the woman as God. In fact, it is not strange at all because the homiletic and artistic tradition has presented the stories this way. It has correctly called our attention to the metaphorical quality of the story about the woman by emphasizing the metaphorical "is not," i.e., that the woman is not God and God is not a woman; but it has encouraged us to literalize the masculine metaphor of the shepherd, to think of the man as God and God as a man.

Another of Jesus' parables, this time in Matthew's Gospel (Mt 13:33), presents God as a bakerwoman kneading the leaven of the reign of

God into the dough of this world until the whole becomes leavened. This parable so clearly presents God as feminine that some scholars have tried to discredit the parable by maintaining that leaven in Scripture is elsewhere a sign of corruption and the woman in the parable is therefore a demonic figure.[55] However, it is clear from the immediately preceding and parallel story of the man sowing the grain of mustard seed in his field (Mt 13:31–32) that such is not the intent of the parable. Luke picks up this same parable of God the bakerwoman in 13:20–21 where it also appears in tandem with the parable of the man sowing the mustard seed. Again we are led to ask why every Christian school child knows who the sower is but not who the bakerwoman is.

Another passage particularly interesting for our purposes is Matthew 23:37 (par. Lk. 13:34) where Jesus presents himself as a mother hen longing to cuddle her chicks under her wing. As Virginia Mollenkott correctly points out in her book on the divine feminine[56] this self-description of Jesus is not a reflection of his earthly self-understanding but of his messianic identity as representative of God. It is God who longs to draw rebellious Israel to herself in and through Jesus.[57] This feminine self-presentation of Jesus as representative of God should generate serious questions both about whether Jesus experienced the God who sent him as exclusively masculine and about whether the Messiah as such, i.e., the Christ, is correctly conceived in exclusively male terms. We will return to this latter point later.

It is certainly true that the New Testament, like the Hebrew Scriptures, presents God in overwhelmingly masculine imagery. But, by placing on the lips of Jesus himself several important feminine metaphors for God, the Gospels make quite clear that the male metaphors are not to be literalized or absolutized. Again, it is perhaps in what is unexpected, in what cannot be explained by cultural influences, that we find the most important and revelatory aspects of the Word of God. It is not at all surprising, and for that reason not especially revelatory, that God is presented in male terms by, in, and for a patriarchal culture. The female metaphors appear in spite of overwhelming cultural bias. They tell us something very important about God, something we may well not have discovered for ourselves in a male-dominated community, that God is neither male nor female, that God is both feminine and masculine.

The second question raised by Jesus' virtually exclusive use of "father" in his own address to God[58] is whether Jesus experienced God and intended to present God as a patriarchal figure and thus as a legitimation of human patriarchy.

First, it is important to note that Jesus' *addressing* God only as Father (if indeed this is the case since the early Church's practice of calling God father may well have governed the New Testament presentation of Jesus' practice) does not necessarily mean that he *thought* of God only in and through this metaphor. As Raymond Brown points out, Jesus' use in John's Gospel of the *egō eimi,* the divine I AM, as the expression of his revelatory unity of action with the one he called his father suggests that his theological conception of God was derived from the Old Testament divine self-appellations.[59] Mary Collins, in a recent article,[60] cites several contemporary challenges to both Jeremias' conclusions about the significance of Jesus' father-address and to recent uses of Jeremias' position to claim that "Abba-Father" is the normative Christian address to God. However, the fact that Jesus spoke often both to and about God as father raises the question with which we are concerned.

It is certain that Jesus experienced God as parental—but why only as father and not also as mother? I would like to suggest that the basic reason had to do not with Jesus' experience of God's gender but with Jesus' patriarchal culture and the constraints it placed on the revelation of God's redemptive plan for humanity.

Jesus experienced himself as one sent by God to do God's work of salvation in this world. This is especially clear in John's Gospel in which "the sent one" is a quasi-name for Jesus and in which Jesus repeatedly attributes his words, his works, his authority, and his life-giving power to God his father (cf. esp. 5:19–47). C.H. Dodd calls this continuous presentation of Jesus as the son sent by the father a "hidden parable" in the Fourth Gospel.[61] The parable is that of a son who is gradually initiated into his father's trade, apprenticed to his father until such time as he is able to take over the "family business."[62] In John's Gospel it is God who first loved the world and undertook the great salvific work that was begun with the promise in the Garden of Eden. Jesus, the son of God, learns from his father how to love the world and finally carries the divine work of salvation to completion by his paschal mystery. This pervasive parabolic presentation of the integration of Jesus' work into the great salvific plan of God demanded that God be presented as father, that is, as the male rather than the female parent. In the patriarchal culture of Jesus a mother-son relationship could not have carried this meaning because mothers had no independent trades and they did not train their male children for adult work. The cultural constraints under which the mystery of redemptive incarnation took place demanded that Jesus experience himself as son of a divine father in order to describe the unique revelation of which he was the subject just as the cultural constraints of the prophetic period in ancient Israel demanded that God be presented as the male rather than the female spouse.

The question, in other words, is not so much *why* Jesus experienced God as father but *how* he experienced him as father. Jesus certainly did not experience God or think of God as exclusively masculine or he could not have presented God in feminine metaphors. The question is not whether Jesus' use of "father" in direct address indicated that he thought God was male but whether it indicated that he thought of God as a patriarch, i.e., as a divine *paterfamilias* exercising absolute power and authority over humanity.

The first indication of a negative answer to this question is the very form of Jesus' address to God as father. Jesus called God "Abba," a word that originated as a "babble word" originally used by little children but later adopted as an affectionate and respectful way by which adult children also spoke to their fathers.[63] The fact that we hesitate to translate the term, to read it as "Daddy" or "Dad," but prefer to use the Aramaic "Abba" demonstrates how intimately familiar the address is. Against the background of the Old Testament in which God is seldom called father at all, Jesus' usage must have been shocking for his contemporaries. Jesus experienced God as an intimate and tender parent, not as a powerful patriarch.

It is important that Jesus, who knew and

used a number of patriarchal metaphors in speaking about God, is never presented as using any of those metaphors in addressing God. Jesus spoke *of* God as king, vineyard owner, employer, and master of the household, but he spoke *to* God only as father with the single exception of his quotation on the cross of Psalm 22 (cf. Mk 15:34; Mt 27:46) when he experienced himself abandoned by his loving "Abba."[64] But even in this case Jesus did not resort to patriarchal address. He cried out, "My God, my God, why have you forsaken me?" No doubt the origin of Jesus' conception of God as father is the Old Testament presentation of God as father of Israel's kings who were God's representatives among the people. Jesus, as God's representative, claimed God as his father and the New Testament writers explicitly apply the royal father-son metaphor of Psalms 2:7 and 89:26 to Jesus (e.g., Acts 13:33 and Heb 1:5). But the application of the father-son metaphor to Jesus' relationship with God differed in a very important way from its Old Testament prototype because Jesus purified it completely of its royal patriarchal overtones and drew his God image from the non-patriarchal presentation of God as the deeply offended but infinitely forgiving father of Israel.[65]

Although Jesus told many parables in which patriarchal male figures represented God, he told only one in which the character of God as fa-

45

ther is explicitly explored. In the parable of the prodigal son (Lk 15:11–32) Jesus presents the fatherhood of God as the very antithesis of patriarchy. In the parable the older son embodies the patriarchal understanding of social relations. He boasts that he has been a perfect son in the patriarchal household. He has served loyally and has never transgressed a single command of the *paterfamilias* whereas his younger brother, by assuming autonomy, has rebelled against the very principle of patriarchy according to which there is only one adult in any family. But to the older son's fury, the father aligns himself with the younger son. It was the father, after all, who had not only permitted but even enabled the boy's rebellion. Now it is the father who renounces the patriarchal right to punish the rebel and welcomes him home with prodigal celebration. Not only does the father decline the older son's challenge to vindicate the patriarchal principle, he even brushes aside the younger son's confused willingness to re-enter the patriarchal structure by assuming the role of a servant. On the contrary, the father receives the boy as the son he has never ceased to be because God's forgiving love, not human evil, determines God's relationship to humanity. The father, far from asserting patriarchal superiority and privilege, seems to recognize the younger son as his equal, i.e., as an adult. To the father the son's return to the household, like his leaving, is an act of adult freedom. The relationship between them is not one of offended domination to rebellious submission but of freely offered love asking and accepting love in return. The prodigal son, like the sinful woman who entered the house of Simon to wash Jesus' feet (Lk 7:36–50), is one in whom loving repentance and loving forgiveness meet in total defiance of the patriarchal model of justification through law.

Jesus' parable about the father actually constitutes a radical challenge to patriarchy. The divine father, who had been understood as the ultimate justification of human patriarchy, is revealed as one who refuses to own us, demand our submission, or punish our rebellion. Rather, God is one who respects our freedom, mourns our alienation, waits patiently for our return, and accepts our love as pure gift. In the parable God tries to educate the older brother, and through him all disciples who prefer the security of law to the adventure of grace, to the true nature of the God who is love. Not only does Jesus say plainly that God is not a patriarch but he definitively subverts any attempt to base human patriarchy on an appeal to divine institution. The power God refuses to assume over us is surely not given by God to any human being. Since the revelation of God by Jesus the claim of divine sanction for human patriarchy is blasphemy.

Three conclusions can be drawn from this

exploration of Jesus' address to God as father rather than as mother. First, in Jesus' culture the father-son metaphor was the only one capable of carrying the meaning of his integral involvement in the work of salvation originated by God. Second, by his use of "Abba" for God and his presentation of God as the father of the prodigal, Jesus was able to transform totally the patriarchal God-image. He healed the father metaphor which had been patriarchalized in the image of human power structures and restored to it the original meaning of divine origination in and through love. Third, he delegitimized human patriarchy by invalidating its appeal to divine institution.

Jesus' metaphorical attribution of fatherhood to God also laid the foundation for his creation of a new family. Those who called no man on earth father (Mt 23:9), that is, who were subject to no human patriarch, could freely associate themselves in a new community of disciples bound together by faith in Jesus. Even Jesus' mother had to make the transition from blood relationship to faith relationship[66] in order to become a member of this new community. Jesus called his followers to leave family and home and follow him (Lk 14:26). And those who followed him became brother and sister and mother to him (Mk 3:31–35), i.e., his new family who, by his invitation, could also call God "Abba" (cf. Mt 6:9).

As Elisabeth Schüssler-Fiorenza points out, this new family of Jesus has no fathers because it is not a new patriarchal structure.[67] Because God alone is father, in the community of disciples all are equals. Children are to be treated with the same respect as adults; women are equal to men; slaves are the brothers and sisters of their masters; Gentiles and Samaritans sit down to table with Jews. As Robert Hamerton-Kelly observes, Jesus called people away from the constraints of family fate into the free embrace of a new destiny.[68] Although the Church, in its obsession with social acceptance and political safety, soon set aside the liberating message of Jesus and patriarchalized the community of the new age,[69] this sin is not to be traced to the good news that Jesus preached but to the male Church leaders who compromised and even perverted the Gospel for their own ends and continue to this day to oppress women members of the Church.

In sum, Jesus' address to God as "Abba" cannot be construed as a revelation of the maleness of God nor as a divine model for human patriarchy. On the contrary, Jesus' teaching about God as father and his calling together of a new, non-patriarchal faith community of equal disciples constitute a liberating subversion of patriarchy which can no longer claim divine sanction but stands revealed as a sinful human structure.

VI. The Maleness of Jesus

We turn now to a totally different dimension of our problem, namely, the sex of the human being Jesus of Nazareth. While it is certainly true that God has no sex, Jesus does, and the sex is male. This historical fact has been used throughout Christian history to support the conception of the God revealed in Jesus as a male being, to legitimate male claims to superiority in relation to women, and to justify a conception of the male as the norm of humanity in relation to which women are derivative and dependent. If any of these ideas are true, the incarnation can only be seen as an unmitigated disaster for women.

A. *The Incarnation*

Jesus is referred to in creed and cult as the Son of God incarnate, suggesting that the incarnation took place in a male human being because only a male could fittingly incarnate a son. In other words, Jesus is male because the Son of God is male. Jesus' maleness, in such an argument, reveals the maleness of the second person of the Trinity. The implications of this argument, as the Fathers of the Church saw, are strictly heretical. Since the second person of the Trinity differs from the first and the third only in relationship, if the second person is male, so are the other two. But this is to attribute to the divine nature a human limitation, sex.[70] The second person of the Trinity cannot be literally male without making God male. As Ambrose said, " 'Vir' [i.e., male] is a name designating gender; gender however is attributed, not indeed to the divinity, but to the human nature" (*De Fide* III, 10:62).[71] In other words, the second person of the Trinity came to be called "son" because Jesus is male, not the other way around. In any case, neither the divine nature nor any of the three persons are male.

As has been observed often in recent biblical scholarship the Jesus of the Gospels and Pauline literature is frequently presented as the incarnation of the feminine Old Testament hypostasis of God, Holy Wisdom or Sophia. Perhaps the clearest such presentation is the Prologue of John's Gospel (1:1–18), the hymn to the incarnation, in which Jesus appears as the Word made flesh. This Word, who is in the bosom of God from all eternity and through whom all things were made, is Holy Wisdom for whom Solomon, equating Word and Wisdom, prayed: "O God of my ancestors and Lord of mercy, who hast made all things by thy word, and by thy wisdom has formed humanity . . . give me the wisdom that sits by thy throne" (Wis 9:1–4).[72]

Joan Engelsman in her well researched book, *The Feminine Dimension of the Divine,* elaborates the claim that the Jesus of the New Testament is predominantly Holy Wisdom incarnate.[73] Paul, especially in the Corinthian correspondence, presents Jesus as "the power of God and the wisdom of God" (1 Cor 1:24), the one whom God has made "our wisdom, our righteousness, and sanctification and redemption" (1 Cor 1:30). Like Sophia, Christ is present with God from the beginning (cf. Prov 8:22–31) and is sent to Israel (cf. Sir 24:11–34) as savior (cf. Wis 10), protector and preserver of the godly (cf. Prov 4:6). Jesus is Law and Life to those who believe in him as Wisdom was to Israel (cf. Sir 24:23; Prov 8:35). In Colossians 1:15–17, paralleling Proverbs 8:22–31 and Wisdom 7:26, the Pauline author says of Jesus:

> He is the image of the invisible God, the first-born of all creation; for in him all things were created, in heaven and on earth, visible and invisible . . . all things were created through him and for him. He is before all things, and in him all things hold together.

In Matthew's Gospel Jesus is clearly portrayed as Sophia. Like Holy Wisdom in Sirach 6:24–31 whose yoke and fetters become sweet and beautiful to those who seek and learn from her, those who follow Jesus and learn from him will find his yoke sweet and his burden light (Mt 11:28–30). Jesus (or the evangelist) even uses the feminine pronoun in speaking of himself, claiming that "Wisdom is justified by her deeds" (Mt 11:19).

In the Gospel of John the portrayal of Jesus as Wisdom is very clear. In the Prologue, as already mentioned, Jesus is presented as the Word who, like Wisdom, was with God from the beginning and through whom God made all things. The "I am" sayings of Jesus in this Gospel, clearly evoking the divine self-appellation in the Old Testament, also constitute an aretology like that of Wisdom in Proverbs 8:12–33. The Johannine discourses, in structure and content, recall the discourses of Sophia. In chapter 6, the bread of life discourse presents Jesus as the one who, like Sophia in Wisdom 16:20–21, gives the bread from heaven.

The Jesus of early Christian faith, in short, was understood to a large extent as the child, the prophet, the emissary, and even the incarnation of Wisdom. And Wisdom, in the Old Testament, was a feminine figure. Perhaps the preference for the masculine term, *logos,* or word, was necessitated by the fact that Jesus was male. But the biblical femininity of the divinity incarnate in Jesus should obviate any temptation to see the maleness of Jesus as a revelation of divine masculinity. The God who comes to us in Jesus is neither male nor female but, especially because of Jesus, there is at least as much reason to image this God in feminine terms as in masculine.[74]

The final theological issue raised by the maleness of Jesus has to do with his role as the Christ. By his resurrection from the dead, Jesus, as Paul says, became life-giving Spirit (1 Cor 15:45), the principle of life of his body which is the Church. But, as J.A.T. Robinson so well said,

> One must be chary of speaking of "the metaphor" of the Body of Christ. Paul uses the analogy of the human body to elucidate his teaching that Christians form Christ's body. But the analogy holds because they are in literal fact the risen organism of Christ's person in all its concrete reality.[75]

In other words, the Christ is not simply the glorified Jesus, but the glorified Jesus animating his body which is the Church. Christ said to Paul, "Why do you persecute *me*?" (Acts 9:4) because the literal fact is that the Christ is composed of all the baptized. This means that Christ, in contrast to Jesus, is not male, or more exactly not exclusively male. Christ is quite accurately portrayed as black, old, Gentile, female, Asian, or Polish. Christ is inclusively all the baptized.

In baptism women, like men, put on Christ. But women do not thereby become male. Consequently maleness, however constitutive of the historical Jesus, is in no way constitutive of "Christ-ness." If it were women could not be baptized.[76] Neither, of course, could blacks, native Americans, Europeans, or anyone else who did not duplicate the physical characteristics of the historical Jesus. Through baptism women share the identity of Jesus *as the Christ* in exactly the same way and to the same extent that men do. This theological fact points out again the heretical character of the attempt to make maleness a prerequisite for representing the Christ in sacramental activity.

Let us summarize then our findings on the theological issues raised by the maleness of Jesus. First, Jesus' maleness was not necessitated by the maleness of the second person of the Trinity, for the second person shares the divine nature of which sex cannot be predicated. On the contrary, the use of father-son language for the Trinity reflects the influence of the maleness of Jesus and his historically conditioned God-experience on christological speculation. Second, Jesus' maleness does not reveal anything about the sex of the Godhead and therefore says nothing about the status of human maleness. Third, the Old Testament personification of God which most comprehensively influenced the understanding of Jesus in the early Church was the feminine figure of Holy Wisdom, so if Jesus reveals anything about the gender of God, it is certainly not that God is masculine! Finally, the Christ, who is the union of all believers in and with the glorified Jesus who is life-giving Spirit, is neither male nor female exclusively but is inclusively all baptized humanity. Indeed, in Christ there is neither Jew nor Gentile, neither slave nor free, neither male nor female because the Christ-identity transforms all into one body (cf. Gal 3:28).

B. *The Significance of the Maleness of Jesus*

As we have tried to show, the maleness of Jesus is theologically, christologically, and sacramentally irrelevant. But the maleness of Jesus is definitely not irrelevant to contemporary spirituality. By spirituality I mean the lived experience of the faith. It includes both how one relates to God and how one relates to self, others, and the world because of one's relationship with God. In this experiential sphere the maleness of Jesus presents a serious problem for women because the normative human being, the mediator between God and humanity, is irreducibly different from women. In a patriarchal society in which male superiority was accepted by women as well as by men this presented no problem. It made sense that God incarnate should belong to the superior half of the race and that women should be represented religiously, as they were in all other spheres, by a man. However, the fact that a problem did not exist in the past does not necessarily render it trivial or spurious. Just as earlier generations have had to wrestle with the Jewishness of Jesus, women today must wrestle with his masculinity.

Obviously, if Jesus was to be a genuine human being he had to be either a man or a woman. The question for women is why he is a male rather than a female. We have already eliminated one reason, namely, that the God he incarnated was male. Now we must deal with a second widely held assumption, namely, that Jesus was male because God chose the superior form of humanity as the appropriate locus for divine self-revelation. The pattern of Old Testament revelation should long ago have put this male conceit to rest. God explicitly corrected a similar self-serving assumption on the part of the Jews, declaring: "It was not because you are more in number [that is, greater] than any other people that the Lord set his love upon you and chose you, for you were the fewest of all peoples" (Dt 7:7). And Paul applied the same divine logic to the earliest Christians:

> For consider your call . . . not many of you were wise according to worldly standards, not many were powerful, not many were of noble birth; but God chose what is foolish in

the world to shame the wise, God chose what is weak in the world to shame the strong, God chose what is low and despised in the world, even things that are not, to bring to nothing things that are, so that no human being might boast in the presence of God (1 Cor 1:26–29).

God's pattern is to choose the least suitable, the least powerful, the most shameful of human material as the locus for the divine activity in order to make clear that salvific action is truly God's.

It is clear that God did not become human as a man either because God is male or because maleness is divine. But we must still ask why, if female and male humanity are equally fitting material for the incarnation, male humanity was chosen. I would like to suggest that, in a certain sense, Jesus had to be a male in order to reveal effectively the true nature of God and of humanity.

First, Jesus revealed by his preaching and his life the inadequacy of the masculine definition of humanity. Jesus repudiated competition, the exercise of coercive power, all forms of domination and control of others, aggression, and violence. He espoused meekness and humility of heart, peacemaking, non-violence, silent patience in the face of injustice and suffering, recourse to personal prayer in times of difficulty, purity of heart, and a nurturing concern for all, especially the sick, the oppressed, sinners, women, and children. In other words, Jesus delegitimized the stereotypically male "virtues" and the typically masculine approach to reality; he validated the stereotypically female virtues and lived a distinctly "feminine" life-style.

Had Jesus been a woman there would have been nothing revelatory about this way of life; women were expected to live and behave that way. Because he was a man Jesus' choice of lifestyle stood out as a contradiction of the current definition of masculinity and thus of humanity as defined by the dominant male culture. But Jesus, choosing to live out a repudiation of the male value system, was recognized by friends and foes alike as possessing an arresting authority (e.g., Mk 1:28; Jn 11:48). So effective was his stereotypically feminine approach that he was perceived as a threat to both state and Church. Thus Jesus undermined the accepted definition of humanity and challenged both men and women to conversion. He challenged men to abandon both their assumption of human superiority and the grounds upon which they based that claim. And he challenged women to value the traits which they had been taught to despise in themselves because they were despised by men.

Second, by his behavior and his teaching Jesus called for and inaugurated a reform of male-female relationships. Jesus chose women as disciples and apostles (cf. Jn 4:4–42; 20:11–18), taught women as he taught men (Lk 10:39), performed miracles for women (Lk 7:11–17; Mt 9:18–26), praised their faith (Mt 9:22) and accepted their love (Lk 7:37–38). At one point he seems to have allowed the superior religious vision of a Canaanite woman to broaden his own messianic self-understanding (Mt 15:21–28). Jesus defended women's loving service to himself and their ministry to others against the men who questioned, attacked, or belittled them (Mk 14:6–9; Jn 4:27–30). He rejected the reduction of women's worth to their reproductive functions when he corrected the woman who praised his mother for bearing and nursing him with the words, "Rather, blessed are those who hear the word of God and keep it" (Lk 11:27–28). He defended women against arbitrary divorce by invoking the order of creation in which the man as well as the woman was called to marital fidelity (cf. Mt 19:3–9). And he refused to collaborate in enforcing the sexual double standard by defending the woman taken in adultery whose partner in sin apparently had not been accused (Jn 7:53–8:11). Most amazing of all, the risen Jesus appeared first to his women disciples and entrusted to them the resurrection kerygma upon which the Church was founded (Jn 20:11–18; see also Mk 16:9 and Mt 28:9–10).

Jesus' attitude toward women was effectively revelatory precisely because he was a man in a culture which neither permitted nor rewarded egalitarian relations between men and women. The early Church recognized as revelatory and acted upon the highly original vision of Jesus concerning the full personhood and equality of women. The question of whether women could be admitted to full Christian identity and mission through baptism seems never to have arisen despite the fact that there was no Jewish precedent for the religious initiation of women. The stories of Jesus' women disciples, even those stories in which Jesus took the side of women against men, in which women's fidelity contrasted sharply with the cowardice and betrayal of male disciples, and in which women have priority over men in the paschal events, were included in the Gospels. Women in the early Church were teachers and evangelists (cf. Acts 18:26), prophets (cf. Acts 21:9), participants in public worship (1 Cor 11:5), and probably leaders of house churches (cf. Rom 16:1; Col 4:15).[77]

Despite patriarchal retrenchment and eventual male repression of women's participation in Church leadership, the message of Jesus recorded in the New Testament remains a resource for women in their quest for justice and a clear condemnation of the men in the Church who have made void the word of God for the sake of their traditions. Today we would call Jesus a feminist, that is, a person who believes in the full personhood and equality of women and who acts to bring that belief to realization in society and church. It is hard to imagine how Jesus' challenge to revise the oppressive relations between women and men could have been presented by a woman. The most effective denunciation of injustice is that which comes from within the ranks of the oppressors. St. Paul says that Jesus was made sin for us (cf. Rom 8:3; 2 Cor 5:21). Part of the sinfulness he assumed was that of belonging to the oppressor class so as to act from within it to heal the division between men and women.

Third, Jesus definitively undermined patriarchy in a way that was open only to a male in Jesus' society. Although it is still oppressively active in the Church, patriarchy's days are numbered because Jesus destroyed its claim to be divinely instituted and sanctioned. As we have already seen, Jesus subverted patriarchy by his presentation of God as a non-patriarchal father. But Jesus' personal choice of celibacy was an equally eloquent statement. In Jesus' society a man entered into the male privileged class by marrying and thereby becoming the head of a family. Jesus renounced participation in patriarchal privilege. He did not take possession of a woman and thus he remained free to relate to all women as equals. He did not have children, so he felt no need to dominate them and so teach them their place. Only as a man could Jesus repudiate patriarchy by his own choice not to legitimate it by participation.

The maleness of Jesus was certainly not an exaltation of masculinity or a revelation of the sex of God. On the contrary, Jesus accepted membership in the oppressor class of society in order, from within, to demonstrate the bankruptcy of the dominative social system. Only as a man could he have subverted the accepted definition of masculinity, validated the so-called feminine virtues despised by men but dear to God, redefined the relationship between women and men as one of equality and mutuality, and destroyed patriarchy's claims to divine sanction.

C. The Spirituality of Women and Men in Relation to a Male Savior

The final problem raised by the maleness of Jesus concerns the relationship of contemporary women and men Christians to the glorified Jesus who indwells us, uniting us with God and with one another in the Spirit. Our encounter with Jesus in prayer is mediated, to a large extent, by the scriptural account of the historical Jesus who is a male human being. Some scholars have suggested, in the light of Jesus' "feminine" life-style and value system, that the historical Jesus is best understood not as exclusively masculine but as androgynous, that is, as both masculine and feminine.[78]

For two reasons this does not seem to be a very satisfactory solution. In the first place, the very idea of androgyny as a characterization of a concrete individual depends on the perpetuation of male and female stereotypes. Thus an androgynous person has masculine traits such as intelligence, power, and initiative and feminine traits such as tenderness, compassion, and intuition. Androgyny may blur sexual identity but it brings us no closer to a conception of full humanity, possessed by both men and women, as embracing all those traits stereotypically divided between the sexes.[79]

Second, Jesus can only be an androgynous *male*. Thus, he would demonstrate that men are capable of assuming everything feminine that is positive or desirable but not that women can assume positive masculinity. It is not to anyone's advantage to add one more male appropriation of feminine value to the long history of literal and figurative rape that women have endured at the hands of men. An androgynous Jesus would establish androgyny itself as normatively male.

It seems to me that our relationship with Jesus, if it is to be authentic, must take seriously both the sex of Jesus and our own sex. Human sexuality is both a perfection and a limitation. A woman, as woman, has access to a range of human experience which is not available to a man. By the same token, being a woman excludes one from a range of experience to which only men, as men, have access. Jesus shared in both the perfection and the limitation of human sexuality, and our relationship with him is governed by our mutual participation in this irreducible human fact.

In practice, this means that women can relate to Jesus in ways men cannot naturally or authentically relate to him. A woman has a sister-brother relationship with Jesus. To a woman the contra-sexual dimensions of the man-woman relationship can enter naturally into her relationship with Jesus. A woman can experience that mysterious maternity toward Jesus which he himself recognized when he said that his disciples were "brother and sister and mother" (Mk 3:35) to him. On the other hand, women do not have access to the relationship between brothers or the man to man relationship with its particular potential for experiencing Jesus as sexual role model.

Historically, the potentialities and limitations which sexual identity imposes upon the relationship between Jesus and his disciples has been seriously distorted by the masculinizing of all human experience. Because God was imagined as a great patriarch in relation to a subordinate humanity, all people were imaged as feminine,[80] that is, as weak, worthless, and sinful in relationship to God. As the Freudian psychologist Ernest Jones put it, men win the approval of a male God by adopting a feminine attitude toward him. "Peace of mind is purchased by means of a change of heart in the direction of a change of sex!"[81] What Jones called "sublimated homosexuality" has seemed a spiritual requirement for men who loved Jesus with a tenderness and passion that a patriarchal and homophobic culture permitted only to women. Much of the most beautiful mystical literature celebrating the marriage of the soul with Jesus has come from the pens of male mystics who experienced themselves as the bride. There is something quite valid in the realization that total receptivity is the basis of mutuality in love. The problem has been in defining such receptivity as exclusively feminine and divine self-gift as exclusively masculine.

Women, on the other hand, because of their femaleness, have often experienced an alienation from Jesus who seemed both utterly different from them and a participant in the oppression of women. Jesus, in his masculinity, has sometimes seemed to be the final divine legitimator of male claims to superiority, the unanswerable argument for the normativity of maleness and the inferiority of women in the divine plan for the human race. Nothing could be more false, and women mystics have gained privileged access to this truth. Not only have they experienced the height and depth and length and breadth of loving mutuality with the divine spouse, a mutuality which requires no sublimated renunciation of their own sexual identity, but they have also experienced the mysterious spiritual femininity of Jesus who gives birth to his Church from his own opened side and feeds his disciples from his own body, thus mystically revealing the special God-likeness that women enjoy through their capacity to give life.[82]

CONCLUSION

The investigation of the gender of God in the New Testament as it is experienced by Christians, especially women, has clarified several issues.

1. The God of the Old Testament is not exclusively male and the father metaphor for God in the Old Testament does not convey a patriarchal God.

2. The God of Jesus is not exclusively male and the one Jesus called "Abba" is not a patriarch.

3. The Christ is a corporate person who is fully present in each of the baptized and who

must be understood as inclusively human, appropriately represented by any of the baptized.

4. The maleness of Jesus is not a revelation of the maleness of God nor of the divinity of males but a free self-emptying by which he participated in the oppressor class of humanity, thereby definitively undermining not only patriarchy but all the forms of oppression derived from it.

5. The historical Jesus of the Gospels through whom our relationship with the glorified Jesus is mediated is male, and this irreducible historical fact establishes his solidarity with us in the experience of sexuality as both perfection and limitation. It also shapes our relationship with him according to the potentialities and limitations of his and our sexuality.

Two conclusions which flow from these realizations are (1) the importance of restoring the feminine to the deity, i.e., of seeing God as feminine as well as masculine, and (2) the urgency of the call to conversion that Jesus, in his masculinity, addresses to both men and women.

The restoration of the feminine to God cannot fail to have beneficial effects on the spirituality of both women and men. First, as Diane Tennis writes,

> The image of the female God makes women fully human, which in turn promotes equal-

68

ity of the sexes. The presence of feminine divinity in the tradition helps legitimate that tradition as credible religion.[83]

It will thereby make it possible for women to experience themselves as able to participate in this tradition without compromising their integrity.

Second, the introduction of femininity into the Trinity not only enriches our conception of God but helps make the Godhead a model for mutual and egalitarian relationships between men and women.[84]

Third, the experience of God as feminine can help heal the relationship of both women and men with God. As Janet Morley insightfully observed,[85] women who experience God only as masculine can easily excuse themselves from the challenge of spiritual adulthood. Female children in our society tend to remain always "daddy's little girl" whereas mothers expect their daughters to grow up. On the other hand, men often fail to negotiate that passage to adulthood which consists in coming to terms with the mother who remains an ever-numinous presence threatening the male with dark possibilities. Although for different reasons, both women and men need to encounter the feminine God. Only a healing of the patriarchal imagination can make this possible.

The second conclusion which flows from our

reflections on the gender of God and the sex of Jesus is that both men and women are called to conversion. Men are challenged by Jesus to reject the cultural definition of masculinity as well as all the patriarchal structures and behaviors which flow from it. In Jesus they have the assurance that there is another, and truly redemptive, way to be a man. Women are challenged to develop a renewed sense of themselves as adult children of God made in the divine image, as sisters and friends of Jesus who have put on Christ and who are called and empowered to represent Christ in Church and society. The traits and virtues which women have experienced as marks of inferiority need to be seen in the light of the life-style of Jesus who validates them and proposes them to both men and women as the praxis of the reign of God.

All of the preceding theological affirmations are important for clarifying our ideas about God and about Jesus. But, as was mentioned at the outset of this essay, it is not primarily abstract ideas which affect our spirituality, that is, our experience of and with God. Important as correct ideas about God may be, it is the imagination which governs our experience of God because it is the imagination which creates our God-image and our self-image. Consequently, if the demonic influence of patriarchy on the religious imagination is to be exorcised, if the neurotic repression of the feminine dimension of divinity is to be overcome, the imagination must be healed. It is absolutely imperative that language, which appeals to the imagination through metaphor, symbol, gesture, and music, be purified of patriarchal overtones, male exclusive references to God, and the presentation of male religious experience as normative. We must learn to speak to and about God in the feminine; we must learn to image God in female metaphors; we must learn to present the religious experience of women as autonomously valid. The therapy of the imagination is an affair of language in the broad sense of the term, and it is crucial that we cease to trivialize this issue and begin the long process of conversion from the idolatry of maleness toward the worship of the true God in spirit and in truth.

1. Sister Mary Madeleva Wolff, CSC, *My First Seventy Years* (New York: Macmillan, 1959), pp. 114–118.
2. See Elizabeth A. Johnson, "The Incomprehensibility of God and the Image of God Male and Female," *Theological Studies* 45 (1984) 441–465.
3. Gregory of Nazianzus, "The Third Theological Oration—on the Son," *Christology of the Later Fathers,* Vol. III, ed. E.R. Hardy (Philadelphia: Westminster, 1954), p. 171. Migne, *Patrologia Graeca* 36:93–96.
4. The argument that priests had to be male to represent Christ is found in Bonaventure. See J. Rézette, "Le sacerdoce et la femme chez Saint Bonaventure," *Antonianum* 51 (1976) 520–527.
5. *Acta Apostolicae Sedis* 69 (1977) 98–116; E.T. *Women Priests: A Catholic Commentary on the Vatican Declaration,* ed. L. and A. Swidler (New York: Paulist, 1977), pp. 37–49.
6. See the excellent article by R.A. Norris, Jr., "The Ordination of Women and the 'Maleness' of Christ," *Supplementary Series of the Anglican Theological Review* 6 (June 1976) 69–80.
7. Norris, "The Ordination of Women," p. 70.

8. Gregory of Nazianzus, "Epistle 101," Hardy, *Christology*, p. 218. Migne, *P.G.* 37: 181.

9. Norris, "The Ordination of Women," p. 74.

10. See Gail R. Schmidt, "De Divinis Nominibus: The Gender of God," *Worship* 56 (1982) 117–131, for a discussion of how male God language affects liturgical experience.

11. See, for example, the article by Carol P. Christ, "Why Women Need the Goddess: Phenomenological, Psychological, and Political Reflections," in *Womanspirit Rising: A Feminist Reader in Religion*, ed. C.P. Christ and J. Plaskow (San Francisco: Harper and Row, 1979), 273–287.

12. Cf. Suzanne J. Kessler and Wendy McKenna, *Gender: An Ethnomethodological Approach* (Chicago: University of Chicago, 1985).

13. On this subject, see Mary Collins, "Naming God in Public Prayer," *Worship* 59 (1985) 291–304.

14. Caroline W. Bynum, *Jesus as Mother* (Berkeley: University of California, 1982).

15. See R. Hamerton-Kelly, *God the Father: Theology and Patriarchy in the Teaching of Jesus* (Philadelphia: Fortress, 1979), pp. 55–60, for a good description of patriarchy in the Judaism of Jesus' time as well as in the Greco-Roman world of first century Christianity.

16. See W.A. Visser't Hooft, *The Fatherhood of God in an Age of Emancipation* (Geneva: World Council of Churches, 1982), esp. chapters one to three, for a fuller description of this social system.

17. Visser't Hooft, *Fatherhood,* p. 2.

18. See Rosemary Ruether, "Feminists Seek Structural Change," *National Catholic Reporter* 20 (April 13, 1984) 4–6.

19. E.g., G. Kaufman, *The Theological Imagination: Constructing the Concept of God* (Philadelphia: Westminster, 1981); R. Hart, *Unfinished Man and the Imagination: Toward an Ontology and Rhetoric of Revelation* (New York: Herder and Herder, 1968).

20. E.g., P.W. Collins, *More Than Meets the Eye: Ritual and Parish Liturgy* (New York: Paulist, 1983).

21. E.g., John Shea, *Stories of God: An Unauthorized Biography* (Chicago: Thomas More, 1978) and *An Experience Named Spirit* (Chicago: Thomas More, 1983)

22. G.B. Caird, *The Language and Imagery of the Bible* (Philadelphia: Westminster, 1980), p. 133.

23. Caird, *The Language,* p. 32.

24. See Werner H. Schmidt, *The Faith of the Old Testament: A History,* tr. J. Sturdy (Philadelphia: Westminster, 1983), pp. 58–60; Dennis J. McCarthy, "Exod 3:14: History, Philology,

Theology," *Catholic Biblical Quarterly* 40 (1978) 311–322.

25. See Virginia R. Mollenkott, *The Divine Feminine: The Biblical Imagery of God as Female* (New York: Crossroad, 1983), pp. 36–43.

26. J.T. Forestell, "Proverbs," *Jerome Biblical Commentary* (Englewood Cliffs: Prentice-Hall, 1968), p. 495.

27. T.H. Weber, "Sirach," *JBC,* p. 541.

28. A.G. Wright, "Wisdom," *JBC,* p. 556.

29. Joan C. Engelsman, *The Feminine Dimension of the Divine* (Philadelphia: Westminster, 1979), esp. pp. 32–41.

30. See the very interesting work of Walter J. Ong, *Fighting for Life: Contest, Sexuality, and Consciousness* (Ithaca/London: Cornell University Press, 1981) on this topic.

31. Caird, *The Language,* p. 132.

32. See the extended treatment of the feminine metaphors in Virginia R. Mollenkott, *The Divine Feminine: The Biblical Imagery of God as Female* (New York: Crossroad, 1983).

33. See Sallie McFague, *Metaphorical Theology: Models of God in Religious Language* (Philadelphia: Fortress, 1982), pp. 145–192, for an extended treatment of the literalization of the father metaphor for God.

34. McFague, *Metaphorical Theology,* pp. 32–42.

35. Johanna Bos, "When You Pray Say Our Father," *Presbyterian Survey* (May 1981), p. 12.

36. See St. Augustine, *On the Trinity* XII, 7, 10. Migne, *Patrologia Latina* 42, 1003–1004.

37. I am indebted to my colleague, Dr. John Endres, and to Dr. Alice Laffey of Holy Cross College, Worcester, Massachusetts for their help on the Old Testament section of this paper.

38. Cf. McFague, *Metaphorical Theology,* pp. 145–192; Bos, "When You Pray," p. 12.

39. Bos, "When You Pray," p. 12.

40. Cf. Diane Tennis, *Is God the Only Reliable Father?* (Philadelphia: Westminster, 1985), esp. pp. 82–83.

41. See Phyllis Trible, *God and the Rhetoric of Sexuality* (Philadelphia: Fortress, 1978), pp. 34–56, and "Feminist Hermeneutics and Biblical Studies," *The Christian Century* 99 (Feb. 3–10, 1982) 116–118.

42. Mayer I. Gruber, in "The Motherhood of God in Second Isaiah," *Revue Biblique* 90 (1983) 351–359, challenges Trible's interpretation.

43. It is interesting that John Paul II in his encyclical *Dives in Misericordia* (Nov. 13, 1980) has a long footnote (#52) in which he explores the feminine significance of *rahamīm.*

44. Cf. Bos, "When You Pray," p. 12.

45. Cf. T. Drorah Setel, "Prophets and Pornography: Female Sexual Imagery in Hosea," *Feminist Interpretation of the Bible,* ed. Letty M.

Russell (Philadelphia: Westminster, 1985) 86–95.

46. See Phyllis Trible, *Texts of Terror: Literary-Feminist Readings of Biblical Narratives* (Philadelphia: Fortress, 1984) for evidences of the male attitude toward women and their rights.

47. R.E. Murphy, "Canticle of Canticles," *JBC,* p. 506.

48. See P. Benoit, "Rabbi Aquiba ben Joseph: Sage et héro du Judaisme," *Revue Biblique* 54 (1947) 54–89; A. Lacoque, "L'insertion du Cantique des Cantiques dan le canon," *Revue d'Histoire et de Philosophie Religieuses* 42 (1962) 38–44.

49. N.K. Gottwald, "Song of Songs, *The Interpreter's Dictionary of the Bible,* vol. IV, ed. G.A. Buttrick *et al.* (New York/Nashville: Abingdon, 1962), pp. 421–422.

50. Origen, *The Song of Songs: Commentary and Homilies,* tr. R.P. Lawson [Ancient Christian Writers 26] (Westminister/London: Newman/Longmans, Green, 1957). Migne, *P.G.* XIII, 17–218.

51. Phyllis Trible, *God and the Rhetoric of Sexuality,* pp. 144–165

52. A. Néher, "Le symbolisme conjugal: expression de l'histoire dans l'Ancien Testament," *Revue d'Histoire et de Philosophie Religieuses* 34 (1954) 30–49.

53. J. Jeremias, *Abba: Studien zur neutestament-lichen Theologie und Zeitgeschichte* (Göttingen: Vandenhoeck & Ruprecht, 1966). E.T. of important sections: *The Prayers of Jesus* [Studies in Biblical Theology, sec. ser. 6] (Naperville: Alec R. Allenson, 1967.

54. Johnson, in "Incomprehensibility," pp. 457–460, alerts the reader to the dangers of treating the Holy Spirit as feminine in contradistinction to the other two "persons" considered as masculine.

55. Cf. Mollenkott, *The Divine Feminine,* pp. 79–80.

56. Mollenkott, *The Divine Feminine,* pp. 92–96.

57. The first "Original Eucharistic Prayer" of the International Commission on English in the Liturgy, May 1984, evokes this metaphor for God: "As a mother tenderly gathers her children, You . . . " (lines 19–20).

58. See J. Jeremias, *The Central Message of the New Testament* (New York: Charles Scribner's Sons, 1965), p. 17.

59. R.E. Brown, *The Gospel According to John,* vol. I [Anchor Bible 29] (Garden City: Doubleday, 1966), pp. 533–538.

60. Mary Collins, "Naming God in Public Prayer," *Worship* 59 (1985) 291–304.

61. C.H. Dodd, "Une parabole cachée dans le quatrième évangile," tr. A. et E. Trocmé, *Re-*

vue d'Histoire et de Philosophie Religieuses 42
(1962) 107–115.

62. See Jeremias, *The Central Message*, pp. 22–27.
63. Cf. Hammerton-Kelly, *God the Father*, pp. 71–73.
64. Cf. Bos, "When You Pray," p. 10.
65. See Jeremias, *The Central Message*, pp. 9–17, on the non-patriarchal father metaphor in the Old Testament.
66. Cf. *Mary in the New Testament*, ed. R.E. Brown, K.P. Donfried, *et al.* (Philadelphia/New York: Fortress/Paulist, 1978), p. 287 and elsewhere.
67. Elisabeth Schüssler Fiorenza, *In Memory of Her: A Feminist Theological Reconstruction of Christian Origins* (New York: Crossroad, 1983), p. 147.
68. Cf. Hammerton-Kelly, *God the Father*, pp. 64–70.
69. Schüssler Fiorenza, *In Memory of Her*, pp. 251–342.
70. Norris, "The Ordination," pp. 75–76.
71. Migne, *P.L.* XVI, 602.
72. Cf. Brown, *Gospel of John*, pp. 521–523.
73. Cf. Engelsman, *The Feminine Dimension*, pp. 107–118.
74. Cf. Schüssler Fiorenza, *In Memory of Her*, pp. 130–140 on Jesus/Sophia.
75. J.A.T. Robinson, *The Body: A Study in Paul-*

ine Theology (Chicago: H. Regnery, 1963), p. 51.

76. Cf. Norris, "The Ordination," pp. 76–77.
77. Schüssler Fiorenza, *In Memory of Her,* pp. 160–204.
78. Cf. D. Gelpi, *The Divine Mother: A Trinitarian Theology of the Holy Spirit* (Lantom: University Press of America, 1984), pp. 232–233.
79. Tennis, *Is God?* pp. 97–99.
80. Cf. C.S. Lewis, "Priestesses in the Church?" in *God in the Dock: Essays on Theology,* ed. W. Hooper (Grand Rapids: Eerdmans, 1970), p. 239: "we are all, corporately and individually, feminine to Him."
81. E. Jones, *Essays in Applied Psycho-Analysis* (London: Hogarth, 1951) 2:366–367, cited in Engelsman, *The Feminine Dimension,* pp. 37–38.
82. Cf. Julian of Norwich, *Showings* 58–63, tr. E. Colledge and J. Walsh (New York/Ramsey/Toronto: Paulist, 1978), pp. 293–305.
83. Tennis, *Is God?* p. 80.
84. Engelsman, *The Feminine Dimension,* p. 156.
85. Janet Morley, "In God's Image?" *Cross Currents* 32 (Fall 1982), 308–315.

SANDRA M. SCHNEIDERS, I.H.M., S.T.D., is associate professor of New Testament Studies and Christian Spirituality at the Jesuit School of Theology and the Graduate Theological Union, Berkeley, California. She has been a member of the Sisters, Servants of the Immaculate Heart of Mary, Monroe, Michigan, since 1955. She is author of *New Wineskins* (Paulist Press) and *Spiritual Direction* (NSVC) as well as more than fifty articles in books and journals.